G. A Moss, T. J Ambrose

The Dutch Rabbit

How to house, feed and breed

G. A Moss, T. J Ambrose

The Dutch Rabbit
How to house, feed and breed

ISBN/EAN: 9783337149420

Printed in Europe, USA, Canada, Australia, Japan

Cover: Foto ©Andreas Hilbeck / pixelio.de

More available books at **www.hansebooks.com**

DUTCH RABBIT:

HOW TO HOUSE, FEED & BREED.

BY

G. A. MOSS,

WITH

CHAPTERS ON COLOUR, DUTCH PAST AND

PRESENT, TYPE, AND TRIMMING

BY

T. J. AMBROSE.

———✳———

IDLE, YORKS.:
PRINTED AT "FUR AND FEATHER" OFFICE.
1897.

IDLE, YORKS.:

PRINTED AT "FUR AND FEATHER" OFFICE.

CONTENTS.

CHAPTER I.

Introduction.

Having been asked by the editor of Fur and Feather if I would write my experiences on this most beautiful variety of Rabbit, and also having received several letters from fanciers in different parts of the country asking me to become one of the authors of the Fancy, I have at last reluctantly complied with their request. The reason of my hesitation was because I am sure there are many others more able to give advice than I am. However, that such advice is being craved for by hundreds of young fanciers is an undoubted fact, and I may say it is the knowledge of this that has spurred me on in this direction, and if I can only feel I have assisted one young fancier in the smallest degree I shall be amply repaid for all my pains.

In this little work I shall deal with the following questions in their respective parts:—Housing and feeding; selection of breeding stock; breeding; and exhibiting. Before I say anything with regard to the above, I should like to point out a few facts which may be useful to some and interesting to others. There is not the least doubt but what there is a very great difference between the Dutch Fancy of to-day and that of eight or ten years back; in

fact, the alteration during this last two or three years is of
a very marked degree, and I believe I can say, without any
fear of contradiction, that no one section of the Rabbit
Fancy has grown so fast, and gained so much favour
amongst fanciers, as our merry little Dutchmen; and if it
were not for that one great question—I fancy I can hear
someone saying "Ah now you are getting at it"—well, the
question of faking—now you have it. If it were not for
this, I say, the Dutch Fancy would have been twice the
size it now is. Thanks, however, to our worthy judges, and
the help of a few sterling fanciers who have set their foot
firmly on the faking business, the time is now come when
cases of this sort are few and far between, therefore, I hope
we may look for a better state of things in the future.

The Dutch Club has certainly done much good work
in this direction, and I would urge all who are in, and
those about to commence in, the Dutch Fancy to join the
club, and help it on in the work it is now doing, not only
in the above question, but also in getting proper classification at shows, &c. For instance, compare the classes
given at shows for Dutch ten years back, when we used to
get one, and, at the most, two classes. Now we have our
six, ten, and fourteen classes provided. Is not all this
ample proof that this most charming variety of Rabbit is,
and will become, more and more popular in the eyes of
honest men?

Perhaps it may be interesting to present-day members
of the Club to know a little of its past history. It was in

"Black Bess," Black Dutch Doe.

The property of Messrs. Wallis & Son, Cambridge.

Winner of 1st and Specials at Hyde, Northampton, Barnetby, Boston, Ossett, Cambridge, Shipston-on-Stour, etc., and Medal for the best type at the Sheffield Dutch Show.

1887 that I first became attached to the Dutch Club; and I believe it was in this year that Messrs. Graham, Outhwaite, Gilpin, and others started the Club, with Mr. Outhwaite as Secretary. I have still the list of members and rules, of that time, by me. In the year 1889 Mr. Graham, I think, took up the secretaryship, and at once went into the matter of revising the rules and the general management of the Club. During Mr. Graham's term of office he did a great deal in the way of getting better classification, &c. When Mr. Graham left Huddersfield for Edmonton he gave up the office of Secretary, Mr. Waller taking it up, and after working it for about two years, resigned. It then came to my turn to have the post, which I have now held for about three years, and I am pleased to say at the present time our Club is in a very prosperous and flourishing condition. It possesses a good cash balance, and a list of members numbering over 200. I have now almost had my little say in this direction, and, in conclusion, I would say to all about to embark in the Rabbit Fancy: Give the little Dutchman a trial, and I feel convinced that if you start in the right direction it will gain so much favour with you that you will find it utterly impossible to leave so fascinating a Fancy.

The Dutch Fancy can boast of many good and true fanciers, men who have done much to improve its tone and raise it to a higher position, viz., first and foremost. Amongst these are Messrs. Ambrose, Malley, Graham,

Tarbox, Enfield, Minkley, Dowson, Wallis & Sons, Robinson, Milnes, Hampshire, Townsend & Grasby, Holroyd, Todd, Cole, Goldthorpe & Son, Harris & White, Freeman & Smith, Marshall, Ball, Senior & Hudson, W. H. King, Philps, Perrin, Bexson, G. & H. B. Smith, Charvil & Mills, Brown, Perkins, Yardley, Levey, Tindall, Aconley, Hudson Bros., Moore, Winn & Moore, Orton, Collyer, Bullock, Boakes, W. King, Rhymer, Adcock, A. and H. Walker, Hooson, Pollard, Bellamy, Pallett, Bleathman, Sanders, Lord, Armstrong, Abbott, Lord & Son, Jennings, Brown, Bownes, Tottle, Stead, Potter, Almgill, Johnson, Woolston, Waller, Blower, Whymark, Wooton & Filer, Legg, Taylor, Clark, Bullock, Bostock & Robinson, Gerry, Prowse, Hoskin, Auckland, Powell & Sharples, Pickering, and many others whose names do not readily occur. I can hear someone saying, "Get on, and let us hear what you have to say in the way of keeping Dutch."

CHAPTER II.

Housing.

In commencing this the first of the practical chapters of my little book, I may say that all that is written herein has been gained from personal experience, and not from mere fancy of the thing, also that it is intended for young fanciers, and not for the old hands, who I do not expect to be guided by me, knowing they are equally well versed in the matter. I shall not say so very much on housing, because so much has been written on the housing of Rabbits that the subject is generally well understood by the veriest tyro in the Fancy.

However, I will point out a few little experiences of my own in this direction. Of course, as regards housing Dutch, it is not so important a question as it is with their more artificial brethren, Lops. In fact, Dutch will do as well out of doors, if not better, as in a rabbitry, providing they are well protected against the weather, and in good warm hutches, with a good bed of sawdust and hay. I am a great advocate of the use of sawdust, as it keeps the hutches dry and keeps down the smell.

I would say to anyone about to commence in the Fancy, and not in a position to erect a rabbitry, do not by

any means let this hinder you. For my own part I should
never build a rabbitry for Dutch if it were not for my own
convenience. Why I like a proper rabbitry is because I
cannot fancy on a cold winter's night having to stand out
of doors to feed and look to one's stock. I like to have a
place where I can go in and spend an hour or two with my
Rabbits. What greater pleasure can a fancier have than
this? This is, without doubt, the one great point in favour
of a proper rabbitry. Still, again, I would say, if you cannot
have a rabbitry, either for want of space or otherwise, do
not let this trouble you ; but mind that your hutches
which are intended for outside are strong and well made.
If not, your chance of success will be very poor indeed.

I find bacon boxes, well scrubbed out, also large
packing cases used for matches, commonly called twelve
gross match boxes, excellent for making outside hutches.
You can generally buy such very cheap from most grocers,
and for the matter of a few shillings they can be made into
hutches, as they are very strong, and will stand the
weather. If such hutches as these are used, and placed
against a wall, with a covering over the top as a protection
against the weather, there is not the least doubt but what
the inmates will do very well ; in fact, far better than if
kept in some of the so-called rabbitries I have seen, where
the owner could just get in, and every available space
being filled up with hutches. Keeping Rabbits in a place
of this sort, in my mind, is nothing less than cruelty, and
it is in such places as these that all kinds of diseases are

contracted, and one in particular, that horrible disease—snufflés.

If you have a rabbitry at all, by all means have a decent one. My idea of the size of a rabbitry, say to hold twenty to twenty-six hutches, is fourteen feet long, eight feet wide, and from six to seven feet high at the eaves. The hutches for such a place should be three feet long, two feet wide, and two feet high. These should be staged three tiers high, with a space of two or three inches between each hutch, so as to allow a free current of air to pass through between them. I much prefer hutches for inside use being entirely open in front, as the Rabbits can then get plenty of air. In a place of this kind, with plenty of *top* ventilation, your stock, if properly attended to, cannot help but do well. When I say top ventilation, I mean it must be well above the tops of the hutches, as nothing is worse for Rabbits than draughts.

Another great point is cleanliness. The hutches should be cleaned out *twice* at least every week. It is far the best to have certain days for this part of the business, as it is more likely to be done, at least I find it so ; and I assure you it has to be something very important which prevents my Rabbits being cleaned out on their proper days. After having cleaned the hutches properly out, shake about them a little disinfectant—Kocide is very good. Then give them a fair sprinkling of sawdust, and in the winter a nice bed of sweet hay. In the summer I do not use hay, only a little for the Rabbits to eat, as I do not think it necessary.

CHAPTER III.

FEEDING.

We now come to what is, to the Dutch fancier, a very important matter. The success of a stud in a great measure may be made or marred by the system of feeding pursued therein. I have no doubt but what many will disagree with me when I say once a day is often enough to feed Dutch. They will say it is starving them, and done to keep them small. I say, nothing of the kind! I have ample proof that it is not so.

First of all, I will refer you to shows where I have exhibited, and see what the reports say about condition. I do not wish by this to sound my own trumpet, but simply to bear out my statement as being correct. These Rabbits are only fed once a day; in fact, none of mine are fed more, except does with young, which have a little bread and milk in the morning in addition to their daily food. Remember, it is not the quantity of food which is given to a Rabbit which brings it into and keeps it in condition, but the quality of the food and the way it is given which does the trick.

I know plenty of fanciers who simply throw the food in to their Rabbits, without any care, and expect them to

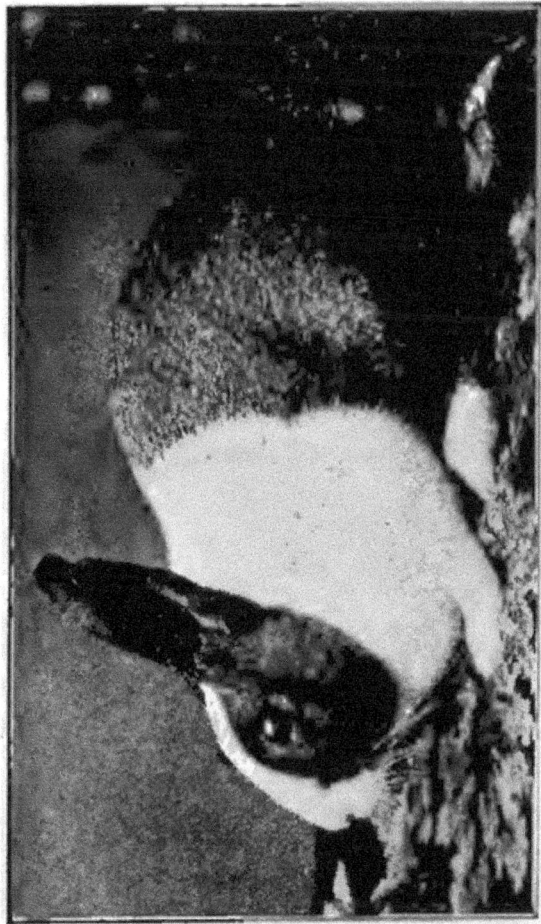

"Oliver Twist," Steel Grey Dutch Buck.

The property of Mr. J. Malley, Hoghton.

Winner of 1sts and Specials Northampton, Haslingden, Burnley, Challenge Cup Sheffield, Edgworth, Darwen, Wakefield, Halifax, Tunbridge Wells.

keep in perfect condition, which, of course, is utterly impossible. If you want your stock to be in good condition, you must study their wants, likes and dislikes. What one Rabbit will eat, another will not touch; and, mind you, it is attending to such things as these which brings success. Above all, see that the food you use is the best money can buy, as it is by far the cheapest in more ways than one. Let your corn, hay, and everything be of the best. Plenty of people think any kind of rough hay will do for Rabbits, but this is a very great mistake. Myself, I am very particular about what sort of hay I use. I do not believe in your dusty, fusty stuff. In the way of corn, I like oats, wheat, and barley, but if I have a choice, it is oats.

We will now suppose you have decided to feed your Rabbits once a day; this is the way I should advise you to go about it, and the way in which my own stock is fed. As to time, I prefer from 7 to 8 p.m. Regularity is a great thing in feeding Rabbits. The first three days of the week give oats, with a nice amount of green food in summer (either chicory, dandelion, hedge parsley, clover, cabbage, &c.); in winter, during the first part of the week, give carrots.

This brings us to the middle of the week, when I always give a nice warm mash, three parts of bran to one part of barley meal, with just a sprinkling of Spratt's Food or Condion, and a pinch of salt. I would advise you to use the barley meal sparingly, as it has a tendency to

make Dutch grow too large. We now come to the latter
part of the week, on which days I should change the corn
from oats to wheat or barley, and in winter, the roots,
from carrots to swede turnips. By so doing, you will be
constantly giving your Rabbits a change of food, a thing
which is most essential, as Rabbits, like ourselves, require
a change of diet.

If at any time you find your Rabbits are off their
food, give a dose of Cholerine as sold by Mr. Knight. It
is an excellent preparation. Sometimes I mix a few tea-
spoonfuls of this wonderful tonic in the boiling water with
which I mix their mashes, and I assure you my Rabbits
very much appreciate it. Another thing which I strongly
advise is giving a drink of cold water daily. I think I
have now said all I have to say with regard to feeding,
and, I am sure, if you adopt the above plan you will find
you are not far wrong, and will not have much trouble in
keeping your stock in good health and condition.

CHAPTER IV.

THE SELECTION OF BREEDING STOCK.

The selection of the first original breeding stock is by no means a small item, but a most important one, that is, if you wish for success. In breeding Rabbits, as in all other animals, it all depends on the way in which you select your breeding stock. I should, therefore, advise anyone about to start breeding Dutch, to pay very great attention to this part of the business. First of all, I should say, make up your mind what colour you intend to breed, be it either black, blue, grey, or whatever the colour may be, and choose your breeding stock according to the colour you are going in for.

I daresay some will say, " What is the man talking about ; why, we can breed any colour of Dutch." To such I say, do not make a mistake, my friend. I know full well it is impossible to breed all colours to perfection, as in trying to get one colour you spoil the other, so it turns out at the finish you have a well-marked youngster, but a poor colour. Then what good is it to you ? None. I would not give a toss up for the best marked Dutch living, unless it was a good colour. " Oh," some will say, "it is markings we want in Dutch, not colour." I am

quite aware we want markings, and, what is more, I am
sure we must have colour.

For instance, visit any show where there is a good
classification for Dutch, and you will soon find out
whether we do not want colour as well as markings.
What we want in a good Dutch is markings, colour, and
type. Either, without the other, is not much good.
Suppose you were judging a class of blacks, and in this
class you find two or three equal in markings, and perhaps
one in this number a beautiful colour, with a coat like jet,
and the others more or less brown in colour, which do you
think would have the winning card? Why, the good
coloured one, of course, would win in a canter ; in fact, I
doubt if it would not win even if it failed a trifle in its
markings to the others, so you see this is where the
question of colour comes in.

In selecting a breeding stock, I strongly advise
choosing a colour as one's ideal, whatever the colour may
be. Of course, I do not wish to infer that by this you will
not breed other colours, which, of course, you will ; but
what I mean is, set your mind on a colour, and try to
improve that colour, not dabble with half-a-dozen colours.
Colour, with me, is a very great point. I love colour. It
is, without doubt, the finishing touch to a good exhibit.
What a pleasure it is to see a beautiful black, with a nice
glossy coat, and how shabby it makes its next door
neighbour look if it happens to be a half-brown specimen.
Therefore, in your breeding stock, keep your eye on colour.

Another important point is type, and a point which fanciers are not paying any too much attention to at the present time, although it is one of the most important points which help to make up a real good exhibition Dutch, and a very taking one in the eyes of a true fancier. We see too many of those long-bodied Dutch. What we want to see is more of the short, cobby, thick-set little chaps. It is not a matter of weight altogether. For instance, a Rabbit only weighing four pounds may not be a good type. I have seen plenty of long, lanky Dutch which would not even weigh so much as this. What you want to do in choosing breeding stock, is to fight shy of these long-bodied Belgian customers, and make up your mind to only have the short, thick sprightly ones. These are always alive, and ready for anything. On the other hand, I find those long, Belgian-shaped ones are nearly always sleepy-looking, so unlike the lively little Dutchman. One of the best type Dutch I have ever seen was the noted steel grey, " Grey Victor," bred and exhibted so successfully by my esteemed friend, Mr. T. J. Ambrose. This Rabbit never lost his shape with age. It seemed rather to improve, and he was always alive to anything, even to having a piece of one's hand or coat. Not a few will will remember "Grey Victor" for this alone. Another Dutch-man, whose type I was very much struck with, was that noted tortoiseshell, " Moonlight," bred by Mr. Singleton, of Dud-ley. Mr. S. exhibited him at Rugby, where he was claimed by Messrs. Hough & Tarbox, for whom he did a lot of win-ning, afterwards passing into the hands of Mr. Townsend.

There is still another point on which I must have
something to say, and to warn young fanciers against,
that is specked, or wall-eyed specimens. These, of all
things, I would strongly advise you to keep clear of in
your breeding stock. Specked eyes is a defect, I am sorry
to say, which is getting very common amongst us, and
what is more annoying to a fancier than when he has a
well marked youngster to find that it has specked or odd
eyes ; because with such a defect the Rabbit is quite
useless for the show pen under a proper judge and in good
competition. As in most other cases, breeders are
entirely to blame for these defects. I quite believe that,
so far as specked eyes go, there is no colour so likely to
throw them up as greys, especially steels, therefore in
breeding this colour, none but those with *perfectly* sound eyes
should be kept for breeding.

I think I am right in saying, in the first place, these
and wall-eyed specimens came from breeding with such
Rabbits as one sees sometimes in a litter of Dutch, which,
but for a few coloured spots here and there, would pass as
a Polish. These Rabbits nearly always have light blue
eyes, such as we should term " wall " eyes in an otherwise
good specimen ; and I have not the least hesitation in saying that if fanciers will breed with such as these we cannot
help having specked-eyed Dutch. I know for a fact many
fanciers say, " Oh ! if you want to breed good Dutch you
must breed from those wasters with only a few coloured
spots on them ; they are the ones to breed winners." I

know better. A few years ago I decided to try it, as I heard so much about this way of getting winners, but, mind you, I kept them clear from my other stock. What was the result? Well, I did not get a Rabbit worth picking up. I don't say but what I had a few good marked ones, but I won't say anything about the colour, and how many white hairs they had in them. After a fair trial I gave up trying to breed winners from such a source. Mind you, I do not mean to say that good ones have not been bred from such Rabbits as these, but they are very few and far between, and what you get into your stock by such breeding takes years to get out. Thus, what you may gain in one way you more than lose in the other. I would strongly advise you to keep clear of such specimens in your breeding operations.

I think I have now made it pretty clear what is wanted, and what is not wanted, in getting together a breeding stock, so we will now proceed a little further, and see which is the best way to get it together. First of all we will suppose that you have decided upon the colour which is to be your ideal. Having hit upon this, I would advise you to get all the stock you require from some well-known fancier, who is noted for the particular colour you intend going in for. Most of our best fanciers have their pet colour, in which they are known to excel. From such a man I strongly advise getting all the stock you may want, as by so doing your Rabbits will hit better together, and your breeding results will be far more satisfactory

than they would be if you got one from one place and
another from another place.   In choosing your does have
them fairly well marked.   Myself, I prefer does for
breeding with good faces, clean necks, and good stops.   I
am not so particular about saddle and undercut.   Having
selected your does, you must then see about the buck,
which should be as near perfect in markings as you can
get him.   If you cannot afford to go in for a good one,
there are always plenty of good bucks at stud in FUR AND
FEATHER, so that you need not be troubled on that score.
Whatever you do in buying stock, find out all particulars,
as to what colour it is bred from, &c., &c., so that you
may know how to pair successfully.   I have now told
you how to go to work in selecting your stock, and in the
next chapter I will have something to say about breeding
the colours.

Mr. Geo. Minkley.

CHAPTER V.

COLOURS.

Under this heading, first of all, I shall deal with the different colours, what stock you require to breed the different colours, and how to pair them to the best advantage. Of course, the leading colour is black, so we will take that first. I myself admire a really good black, and we have no colour which is so popular amongst fanciers, and from time to time many grand specimens have appeared on the show bench. The first crack which I can remember was the noted "La Mode." This was many years ago, then came Mr. Outhwaite's "St. John." Amongst the best of late years, special mention may be made of Mr. F. Tindall's "Magpie," winner of upwards of one hundred prizes; Mr. Malley's "Pinate," also a great winner; and Messrs. Lord & Son's "Lord Rutland." Now we have Mr. Graham's noted "Cleopatra," and Messrs. Wallis's winning black. Amongst others who have *bred* and exhibited good blacks may be mentioned Messrs. Holroyd, Warr, Marsden, Taylor, Smith, Hinson, Ball, Worral, Allison, Havercroft & Son, Weston, Pollard, Bleathman, Levey, Johnston, Naylor, Robinson, Jennings, Bettison, Bowskin, Ottewell, Addy & Son, Stead, &c.

If I were about to start breeding blacks, I should first
of all buy two bucks—a black and a blue. I should then get
as many does as I required of the following colours, blacks,
blues, and greys. The black does should be paired with
the blue buck, and the blue and grey does with the black
buck. I do not believe in pairing two blacks, as these
colours do not hit well together. On no account pair the
blues with the greys, nor any that may be bred from greys,
or you will have too good a supply of "off" colours, as
they are termed, such as blue greys, blue fawns, &c.
There is not any doubt but what these "off" colours are
the result of improper pairing. If, by any chance, your
space is limited, I should advise only one colour being
taken on, either blacks and blues or blacks and greys, as
if all the colours mentioned above are kept, you will have
to keep them each quite separate. Of the two crosses, I
much prefer blacks and blues, as we all know a blue-black
of anything is always the best.

Next in the order of colour come blues. This is a
colour which has been very much neglected, although,
during the last few years it is so very much improved, still
one does not even now see many real good-coloured ones.
The great failing seems to be light ears and white ear tips,
a fault which completely takes away the beauty of the
blue. I must say I cannot endure a blue if not a good
colour, with ears to match the body colour. I am very
much surprised at fanciers not giving more attention to
this charming colour, as I am sure not any of the many

colours we have in our little Dutchmen can be more striking than a real good blue.

As many know, this is my favourite colour. A few years ago I went in for this colour, and succeeded in breeding some very good specimens, both for colour and markings, and I am quite sure if breeders only go the right way to work, good coloured blues can be bred as well as any of the other colours. Mr. Robinson, of Birmingham, has turned out some good exhibits of this colour, one in particular, the noted doe, "Duchess," I believe, was her name, which won for her owner many prizes. Ten pounds was offered for this doe the first time she appeared in the show pen at Birmingham, when quite a youngster. The chief art in breeding blues is to get them to retain their colour. Many are a good colour when they are young, but with a little age go off considerably. Mr. Garlick, of Kettering, has turned out some really excellent blues, and I remember one doe he had a few years ago, which was a splendid colour, and went on winning for several seasons, and when last I saw her her colour was as good as ever. Messrs. Hough & Tarbox exhibited last season a really excellent blue. Chief amongst its winnings were 1st and special for best adult Dutch in the show at Birmingham. This, I believe, is a record win for a blue, and goes to prove that a good-coloured, well-marked blue can hold its own amongst any of the other colours. Amongst others who have had, and exhibited, good blues, may be mentioned —Messrs. Malley, E. F. Ball, Ware and Son, Minkley,

Philps, Marshall, Morris, Wallis & Son, Winn & Moore,
Barraclough, Dowson, Burnett, Weekley, Townsend,
Palmer, Clark, Littlewood & Son, G. & H. B. Smith, &c.

Great difference of opinion exists as to colour. Some
prefer a light blue, others a darker shade. Myself, I like
good deep colour, but, at the same time, bright and glossy.
As to the kind of breeding stock required, I recommend
the following :—First of all, get a blue buck ; make sure
he is a good sound colour, and bred from blacks and blues.
The colour of your does should be blacks, either bred from
blacks and blues, or from blacks and tortoiseshells, and a
tortoiseshell doe or two bred from blacks will not be out of
place. Perhaps some may not be aware that a little tortoise blood will work wonders in improving the colour of
blues. Try it, friends, and if you are not well satisfied
with the results I shall be surprised. I find, besides
deepening the colour, it also makes it last longer.

The next colour in order of merit to blues is, in my
opinion, tortoiseshell, and whatever may be said of all the
beautiful colours of Dutch, no one can deny but what a
tortoise can hold its own with any of them. We all know
the saying, "A thing of beauty is a joy for ever," and I
feel certain that all will agree with me that a real good-
coloured tortoiseshell is a thing of beauty of no mean order,
and one of which any fancier who succeeds in breeding it
may well feel proud. This colour, as with blues, has of
late years fallen off considerably, and has not made the
strides towards perfection it should have done. One seldom

sees a rich bright-coloured tortoise, with nice shadings ; there seems so many of those smudgy, dirty-coloured specimens about. Again, in this colour, we have a *very great* difference of opinion as to the correct colour a tortoise should be.

Some say they should be broken up, the same as a tortoiseshell Cavy, in patches evenly all over the body. I have seen one or two of this kind, and I must say I was very much struck with them. At the same time, my idea of a proper tortoiseshell is exactly the same as was described in FUR AND FEATHER of February 13th, 1896—body colour a rich fawn, with dark shadings running along the sides of the body to the hind quarters, the shading gradually getting darker as it reaches the haunches, running well down the hind legs, where it should be very deep ; the tail the same. The face should be the same colour as the body, with very dark shading round the muzzle, and running along the cheek bones into the ears ; the cheeks should also be nicely shaded, the ears should be of a very dark shade, in fact, almost black. If there is one thing I dislike to see in a tortoise more than another, it is light ears. This is, in my opinion, a *very great fault*. What looks worse than a tortoise with almost white ears ? Yet we see many dozens of them. Why is it ? Surely breeders can do something to remedy this. One thing I am certain of is that light ears are on the increase, and unless breeders pull themselves together, and try to remedy this growing evil, we shall soon lose one of the most striking features of

an ideal tortoiseshell. There is not any doubt but what
a good tortoise is worth having. It is a colour which will
last, if properly bred, and will not fade, as most other
colours do.

For instance, take as a pattern that champion of
champions, " Moonshine," bred by Mr. Bellamy, of
Kettering. He is now, at the time I write, over five
years old, and still he can win. This is ample proof of
what good tortoiseshells can do. Just look at the firsts
and specials "Moonshine" has taken, is it not enough
to make any one's mouth water? I can say more than
many people as regards " Moonshine." I had the
pleasure of seeing him first time he was exhibited. It
was at Rugby, where he was shown in the old class
when about eight weeks old. Soon after this he passed
into the hands of Mr. Pearson, of Hull, at a long price,
who exhibited him most successfully. From Hull he went
on to Huddersfield, to swell the stud of Mr. Smith, and,
last of all, into the hands of that genuine fancier, Mr.
Minkley, of Sheffield. Mr. Minkley tells me he shall
keep him as long as he lives, and I may say
I am delighted to know that this grand old Rabbit
is to end his days in such a good home. Another
noted tortoise, which won upwards of one hundred
prizes, was the noted " Princess," bred and exhibited
by Mr. Robinson, of Birmingham. " Princess May,"
hailing from the same rabbitry, also did a lot of
winning.

Amongst others who have turned out good tortoise-shells may be mentioned — Messrs. Johnson, Malley, Howard & Son, Todd, King, Singleton, Brown, Granger, Holroyd, Orton, Tindall, Jennings, Lord & Son, Hinkley, Gladwell, Beck, &c. As to the kind of stock for breeding tor-toiseshells, I like the following :—A tortoise buck, mind that he is a good bright colour, with nice shading, and quite free from light ears. Also make sure that he has not a lot of white hairs mixed up on his body colour. Many, if well looked into, have this fault, and I strongly condemn such a Rabbit as a stock buck, as youngsters bred from such a Rabbit are sure to throw up a lot of white hairs. They will be a good colour during their first coat, but as soon as they begin to change their baby coat for a new one, white hairs will come in abundance, and then your Rabbit is useless. As to does, they should be blacks, bred from blacks and tortoises, and tortoises bred from the same source, or tortoise does with just a little blue blood in them will not be out of place. If all are of a good colour, and from reliable strain, I have no doubt but what you will get good-coloured tortoiseshells.

We now come to the greys. In these we have several different shades of colour, but I intend only to speak of two, namely, the steel grey and the light grey. In these colours we cannot complain much of neglect, for there is not the least doubt that greys have become very popular of late years. I should say that where ten greys were bred five years ago, there are fifty now. The chief reason for this is

owing to the steel greys making such a stir about that
time ; everyone was simply raging about them, and steels
certainly looked like having it all their own way, and soon
crushing out the poor light shade. However, such was
not to be, and in time the steel grey passion seemed to
wane, and to-day the light shade has by far the stronger
position of the two colours. Of course, everyone will
admit that a real nice-coloured steel grey is a very taking
rabbit, and- it makes the light shade look quite shabby
when side by side. I said *nice* coloured steels : note the
nice, please ; but how many good coloured steels do we see ?
Very few, I am sorry to say. But we see plenty of greys
which it would puzzle the best of us to give a name.
Those with the colour on the body about ten shades darker
than it is on the head, and *vice versa,* one or two different
shades on the body, and dull and cloudy in appearance,
more like half-bred blacks than anything else. Such
Rabbits as these are not steel greys at all, but mere
mongrels, the result of reckless mating. A proper steel
should be one uniform colour, evenly ticked, not too
dark, and the coat should be sharp and bright in appearance.
One of the best steel greys ever penned was the noted
"Eclipse," bred by Mr. Johnson, of Kettering, and sold, when
quite a baby, to Mr. Tottle, of Bristol, at a long price.
Afterwards he came into the hands of Mr. Ambrose, who
exhibited him most successfully. When I first saw him,
which was at Leicester, some six years ago, I must say I
admired him very much, and I believe it was the general
complaint with all fanciers present. It was at this show

that Mr. Graham, who was judging, gave him the cup for the best Dutch—a most popular award. After this he secured the cup at the Palace ; then he left Bristol along with his stable companion, " Grey Victor "—another grand-coloured steel grey—to swell the stud of that much-lamented fancier, the late Mr. Cooper, of Burton-on-Trent, the price paid, I believe, for " Eclipse " being £15. Many were the wins this grand pair of greys did for their owner. After the death of Mr. Cooper, they both went back to their old home (Bristol), but " Eclipse " was not to stay long, Mr. Ambrose soon selling him to that noted Dutch-man, Mr. Malley, for whom he did well.

Amongst other noted steel greys which have done so much winning, may be mentioned Mr. Malley's "Sunbeam," which won over fifty firsts and many other prizes. Messrs. Winn and Moore's " Grey Victoria," Messrs. Wallis and Sons' " Grey Monarch," which has now won 29 firsts and other prizes ; Mr. W. G. Baxter's champion " Grey Duke," which has also gained the Dutch Club champion certificate. This Rabbit is one of the best-coloured steels out at present. The light greys cannot boast of such a successful career ; at the same time many really excellent specimens have graced the show pen. In this shade, Mr. Malley has held a strong hand, time after time putting down some real gems, the one with which he won at the Palace in 1894 being about the best I have seen. Again, at Lincoln, last year, he penned a good one, taking the challenge cup over the steel greys. Mr. A. E. Brown has exhibited a grand-marked Rabbit of this colour ; Messrs. G. & H. B. Smith, of Bedford, have penned some very nice light greys, also Messrs. White and King, of the same town. The one this firm is now exhibiting is, I believe, about the best light shade out. Amongst others who have bred and exhibited good greys may be mentioned Messrs. Minkley, Hough & Tarbox, Goldthorp & Sons, W. & R. Yardley, Orton, Prowse, Hercock, Blower, Benion, Banks, Perkins, Singleton, Bettison, Walker & Son, Bellamy, Brown, Stevenson, &c., &c.

I find the following stock answers well for breeding greys :—A steel grey buck, make sure it is a proper colour, and bred from a good strain. Does :—Blacks bred from black and greys, tortoiseshells and light greys bred from blacks or tortoiseshells. Whatever you do, make sure your stock for grey breeding does not contain any blue blood.

We have now had a glance at the five leading colours in Dutch ; the other colours are not now very much in evidence, but out of what I term other colours, there is one which, I am sorry to say, has, so far as the show pen is concerned, nearly died out, in fact completely so : that is yellow. Why, it is a mystery, as I feel certain no one will dispute the fact that a good-coloured yellow looks very pretty, as well as striking to the eye of the true fancier. I suppose the chief cause of its disappearance is due to its receiving so little encouragement of late years on the show bench ; but now in these days of revised classification, I am sure there is a splendid opening for good yellows, with clear and distinct markings.

If I were about to breed yellows, this is how I should commence. First of all procure a very bright-coloured tortoise buck with shadings as pale as it is possible to get them, and mate him with some good fawn does. From this cross keep the lightest coloured ones, pair them up again, and so on, and in time, with careful mating, I should obtain the desired object. Blue greys and blue fawns I will say nothing about, as I am not at all struck with them, and most fanciers can get them in plenty. Of course, there is no doubt but what a good-marked one of these colours is worth having in these days of large classification. For instance, one of these colours won the cup at Lincoln last year for best Any Colour. As far as colour goes, I have now finished, so we will proceed with our breeding operations.

CHAPTER VI.

BREEDING.

At the start, I must give a caution : do not be in too great a hurry to commence breeding with young does. I generally commence with my does when they are about six months old, not before. Some, I know, begin much earlier than this, four months even, but it is my firm opinion that if you want strong, healthy youngsters, a doe should not be put up for breeding until she is more than six months old, for common sense will tell anyone that a doe younger than this has not strength sufficient to bring up a litter of healthy Rabbits. What good are a lot of weak sickly things to you ? Why, more trouble than they are worth. Some say, " Oh ! we want to keep them small." Well, if this is your plan to keep them small, I say forsake it, and go in for what I said concerning type, and remember it is not altogether the smallest which is the best type. If your does are of proper age, in good coat—not moulting, mind you, never breed with a doe when in moult ; if you do, the youngsters will always be loose in coat- and ready for use, place them in the hutch with the buck, never put the buck into the doe's pen ; if you do a fight may occur. You will then soon perceive if the doe is in use; if so, let her be struck

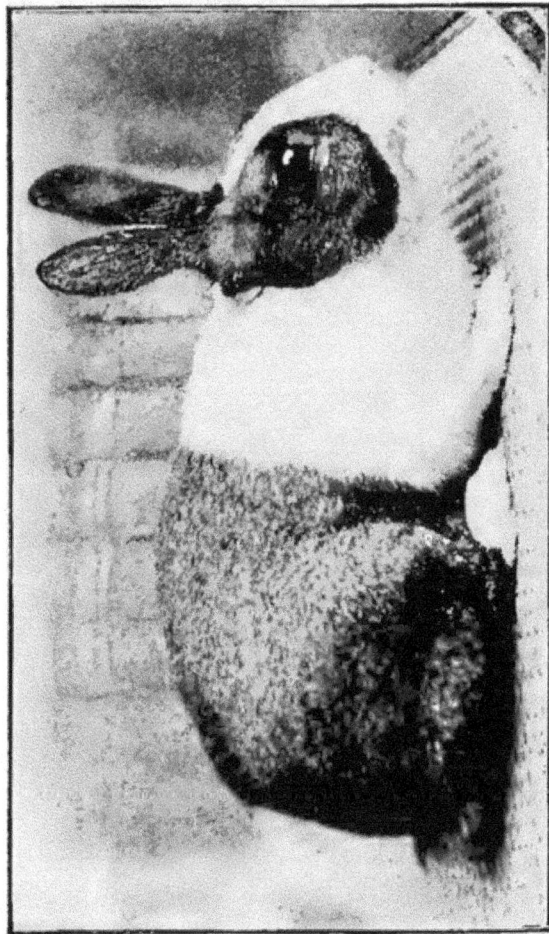

"Grey Victor II.," Steel Grey Dutch Buck.

The property of Mr. W. G. Baxter, Grimsby.

Winner of 1sts and Specials Ossett, Barnetby, Skipton, Stalybridge, Barton, etc.

twice, not more ; then take her away and place her in the hutch where she is to rear her young.

As to the kind of hutch, I myself prefer one with a breeding apartment, although it is not altogether necessary. At the same time I have had does which would not rear their young unless they had a proper breeding hutch. During the time the doe is going in young, she should be well and properly fed, and about three or four days before she is expected to kindle, give her a little warm bread and milk once a day ; also see there is a little water kept in the hutch. If this is attended to, and a good bed of sweet hay given, you may rest assured all will be well. After the doe has kindled, the warm bread and milk should be continued for a few days, in addition to the daily food, after this the ordinary food may be given. As I said in another part of this work, my Rabbits are only fed once a day, except does with young, which have either a little bread and milk or a little green food given in the morning, until the youngsters begin to run about. After this they are only fed the same as the others.

Some fanciers arrange so as to have several does kindle at the same time, they then kill all the young that are not pretty good in markings, and put the best ones all on one or two of the does, putting the other does to the buck again. Of course, as a rule, Dutch are capital mothers, and you can do almost anything you like with their young. I generally have a look at the young ones as soon as the doe has kindled, first of all taking the doe out of the hutch, then, after rubbing my hands with a little hay, I have a look for the eye-opener. I take away the worst marked ones, put a little something tempting in the hutch in the way of green food, then put back the doe. I do not care for the plan of taking all a doe's young from her, as, in the first place, I consider it is cruel, and, secondly, because it makes her lose confidence, particularly if she is a young doe. I like youngsters to run on the doe until they are about six weeks old, by which time they should be taken away, putting the bucks in a hutch to themselves, and the does the same. In doing this do not put too many together, as they will not do so well, also, if too crowded, their ears will grow too long, a bad fault in a Dutchman. If you have one in a litter which, in your opinion, is going to make a winner, let it stay on the doe a day or two after the others are taken away, then, when you do take it away, put it in a hutch by itself, and give it your best attention.

Do not give youngsters too much green food. At the same time, a little, if carefully given, will do them good. After you have taken the doe from her young, do not give but very little green food for a day or two, so as to dry up her milk. Don't be in too great a hurry to put the doe to the buck again, but give her a little time to get up her strength. Myself, I generally commence breeding at the end of November, and between this time and July I expect to get about three litters from my does; about August they begin to go into moult, so from that time until November I always give them a good rest.

As to the age a buck should be before he is put up for breeding, I like mine to be about six months, certainly not younger. Even then for the first six months do not use him too much, particularly if he is an extra good one, and you wish to keep him in show form. At this period, one doe a week, is quite enough. After he has attained the age of twelve months, if properly fed, you may use him to three does a week, if you are not exhibiting him, but if you are exhibiting him regularly he should not be used more than once a week. As to the age a buck will remain good for stud purposes, I find, if properly used, they will last for five or six years. When once you have got a buck that suits your does stick to him ; not go changing from one buck to another every few weeks. Whenever you do introduce a fresh one into your stock be sure you find out all about him, how he was bred, and who by, and from what colour. You must remember a buck plays a very important part in breeding matters. Last, but not by any means least, when you have once got together your breeding stock, stick to it, and not go chopping and changing them about all the time. If you wish to breed winners you must do a little in-breeding. Never mind what others say to the contrary. A properly selected breeding stock, with a little in-breeding, is the secret of success. I have now been through the housing, feeding, and breeding experiences, and as a conclusion to my little work I will give you a few hints respecting exhibiting.

CHAPTER VII.

EXHIBITING.

I may say that lately this is a thing I go in for but very little, only showing at one or two of our best shows, for somehow or other I have taken a preference to selling my stock at home in their own pens. However, during my career in the Fancy I have done a great deal at it; it is now about fifteen years since I exhibited my first Rabbit. During the time intervening I can assure my readers I have seen some ups-and-downs, and many great changes have come upon the Rabbit Fancy. I will, first of all, have a few words to say on does exhibiting pay. I am quite sure many will say *no* ; however, in spite of such an answer, I shall say *it does*, but to make it pay it must be taken up in the proper way. It is no use a young fancier buying a second-rate specimen, and sending it to shows all up and down the country, expecting it to win everywhere it goes, for if he does he must be prepared for disappointments, as he will spend a lot of money, and get very little return. I say to all who intend to exhibit, if you have to buy your stock go in for nothing but the very best. Remember, if you do have to pay a long price for a good

specimen, it will repay its cost, and give you a name in the
Fancy, then you will find exhibiting pay, but a second-
rater will do neither.

Having looked at this side of the question, I will
proceed to say a few words to the fancier who breeds his
own exhibits. Supposing you have had a fair breeding
season, and have a few youngsters which you consider
likely to go out and get into the money, take my advice,
and do not be in too great a hurry to send them out,
however anxious you may be to win a prize. I am well
aware most fanciers like to get a good youngster out as
soon as possible, but I say again, do not be in too great a
hurry, as many good youngsters are spoiled through being
shown too young. For my part, I consider it by far the
best not to send out a good youngster until it is ten or
twelve weeks old, by which time it will be able to stand
the strain of exhibiting. I must, however, admit I, myself,
have shown youngsters younger than this, but whenever I
have done so luck has always been against me, so that I
should have been a lot better off had I kept them at home.
I have a good proof of this in my rabbitry now, which will
be revealed later on. On the other hand I have kept
plenty of Rabbits at home until quite grown up before
showing them. To further substantiate my statements,
I may say I know plenty of fanciers who will not send
out their Rabbits until they are three or four months old.

During a recent visit to Sheffield I saw an example of
this, as, on visiting the rabbitry of one of our best fanciers

in that town, I saw several youngsters which could have
been well in the money at the Dutch Show, and I don't
even know but what one of the number—a tortoise—would
have won the cup, still, our friend would not show them
because he thought them too young. Another thing
which I do not believe in is showing a Rabbit too often.
Some fanciers send the same Rabbit to two or three shows
a week, and keep on doing this week after week. In time
this is sure to tell its tale, as all must admit. A thing I
always do when sending my Rabbits to shows is to put a
little food of some kind into the box with them ; about the
best thing for this purpose is a *ball* of barley meal, bran,
and a little Condion, mixed ; in addition to this I always
give a drink of milk with a teaspoonful of Knight's
Cholerine in it, both before they go and when they return.
By doing this you prevent scours, and bunny is very little,
if any, the worse for its out. One Rabbit I had which
was very fond of milk, used always to be ready for her
pick-me-up when she arrived home from a show, and she
would not settle down until it was given her. I might say
that in the summer I give the milk cold, and warm in the
winter.

Another very important point which many do not
give enough attention to is the travelling boxes. Where
you see one decent exhibition box you may see twenty
very bad ones. This is, without doubt, a very great
mistake, as, in addition to having your stock damaged,
you are much more likely to get them lost, which, in

many cases, is entirely the fault of the exhibitor through bad boxes, &c. Some of the boxes I have seen at shows are nothing short of a disgrace—anyone who has been a steward at a large show knows this to be only too true— lids nailed on in pieces, labels nearly if not quite off; you see all these kind of things at a show, then owners wonder why their stock goes wrong. My advice to all young exhibitors is to have good exhibition boxes, not too small. One of the best boxes I have seen is that made by Mr. Hillyer, of Northampton; they are reasonable in price, well and strongly made, not over heavy, strength and lightness being well combined. Above all see that the labels are securely attached. If you attend to these few points, and the show is under proper management, you will have little cause to complain. One thing more I might add; that is, do not be too late in starting your exhibits. Remember most good shows make arrange- ments to pen all the stock directly it arrives, and if your Rabbits have time to settle down in their pens before judging, they look all the better.

Below I give my standard of the points of perfection. It will be seen that I differ a little in some points with the Dutch Club standard. I have given more points to certain parts, finding, as I do from breeding experience, that such points are by far the most difficult to obtain.

Blaze and cheeks, blaze to be of a nice wedge
    shape, tapering off finely, and running
    through the ears ; cheeks nicely rounded,

well covering jaws, not to run in neck, and to run close down to smellers, but not to touch same...	20 points
Clean neck	10 ,,
Saddle	10 ,,
Undercut	10 ,,
Feet stops, to be from 1 to 1½ inches in length, and cut even on top and underneath ...	20 ,,
Ears	5 ,,
Eyes, free from specks	5 ,,
Type and colour	15 ,,
Condition	5 ,,
Total ...	100

Negative Points.

Small specks on eyes to lose	10 points
Eyes with specks approaching anything near a quarter of the eye to lose	20 ,,
Distinct spots or flesh marks on any part to lose	20 ,,
Over 5½lbs. in weight to lose	20 ,,

Mr. T. J. Ambrose.

CHAPTER VIII.

BREEDING FOR COLOUR.

I have had, from time to time, many opportunities of discussing Dutch breeding, and I have found no subject on which are held so many and varied opinions as this. Each and everyone has different views about breeding for colour. I know the orthodox idea is to secure a black buck, and as far as a stock rabbit goes, you are secure in breeding him with any does you like. This, to a great extent, is correct, as black is no doubt the foundation colour of all, and offers greater facilities than any other colour.

This being the colour most extensively bred, I will deal with the breeding of blacks first, and will say that they are the most difficult to obtain, because the faults are so very apparent ; no colour shows the white hairs on body, the ticking in the ears, or a little white spot on the belly so plainly. The latter is a frequent failing in Dutch. Up in the middle of the thighs the white spot is so readily distinguished in a black, but I have known cases of a fair sized spot go on right through the exhibition life of some colours without being noticed.

In a black, these defects are fatal to its success, and consequently, as I have said, they need the most careful attention.

It is, therefore, an absolute necessity that you should avoid
Dutch for breeding which have really bad ears. I mean
those that are ticked almost like a silver, and especially
those that have flesh-marks ; these generally appear on the
tips, and are almost certain hereditary traits which will be
transmitted faithfully to the progeny. I have always been
struck by the fact that it is far easier to transmit faults
than points of excellence. The one comes with unvarying
regularity, whilst the other is oftimes the work of years
to concentrate. Ticking on ears, and spots on belly should
always be rigorously avoided. Keep the black as solid as
possible. This is what is termed good sound colour.
I know that too much attention can be paid to this ticking,
and in judging too much weight attached to it, because
many exhibitors have a great stock of patience, and this
and a pair of tweezers will, to a great extent, reduce this
fault.

Another great fault, and one that is very frequent with
this colour is the rapidity with which some exhibits go
brown in colour—I have three noted winners on my mind
whilst writing this, " Magpie," Messrs. Wallis's black,
and the black that was shown by Mr. Chappell during
1896.—This has been generally admitted to be the want
of a moult, and rightly so ; but oftimes the real cause is
their having tortoise blood in them, and it is the blending
of brown with the black that causes the brown to
preponderate, get on top, and consequently spoil the
colour. I should therefore in breeding blacks avoid

as much as possible the use of tortoiseshells ; also greys, because of the ticking.

This brings me to the utility of using a good coloured blue as often as necessary, to keep up the standard of colour in blacks. Blacks so bred can be mated black buck and black does for several generations, without any appreciable weakness in the colour. The use of blue blood gets that lovely purple sheen on the top, and great depth of colour so desired by all Dutch-men. I remember several years ago, pairing, as an experiment, two blues which had been bred from blacks, and getting a black buck from the cross, which for purity of colour and brightness I never saw equalled ; and what is still more interesting, he got some wonderfully good coloured youngsters. I should, therefore, always advise the foundation of a stock for breeding blacks to be kept exclusively to the two colours, blacks and blues ; by so doing, one would avoid a lot of trouble, and the improvement in the stock would be marked to such an extent that the owner would never depart from the plan ; at the same time he would, no doubt, get some grand blues from the same cross.

I know many think that I attach far too great importance to these minor details, but I have always held that to be successful in breeding Dutch, one must carefully avoid the rough and ready pairing which takes place on all hands. There is less attention paid to pairing Dutch than any variety of rabbit bred. So much is always left to chance, because some of the cracks have been chance bred, but if a sound basis had been adopted in pairing, I am sure we should have got Dutch with far more even quality in every way. Ask any practical silver breeder if he would indulge in this reckless mating of colours, and he will at once tell you that such is fatal. Until breeders of Dutch recognise their duty in getting their specimens sound and honest in colour, no advance can be made in this direction. I know that all other interests fade in the race for markings, and the other points are considered of little importance. This of course is a natural result in such a variety, but if fanciers would only follow common sense lines, and breed from the colours that will blend well together, the trouble would be no greater, and the result more than repay any trouble or expense they may be put to.

In extending this explanation to general purposes, I do so hoping that it may be giving those who never thought the subject out, the result of my experience; and I shall now only have to deal with the other colours in a manner that is peculiarly adapted to its special requirements, because the general rules are the same—I mean, in avoiding those specimens which have ticked ears and bodies, flesh markings on ears, and spots on belly.

I next take the pairing of blues, and the best mating, of course, is to a black, because in nearly every case the result of pairing blues to blues is fatal to rich, pure colour. It comes far too pale. I have on several occasions used a steel-grey as a cross to increase the depth of colour

on ears, and the result has been most satisfactory, and
I have seen excellent steel greys bred from this cross.
I hope more attention will be paid to this colour, so that
they may be got with greater depth of colour, and brighter
on top, with special attention paid to the ears—the
stumbling block to most breeders. In recommending the
steel grey cross, I know that the result will be a few blue-
fawn and blue-grey youngsters. I should not recommend
any fancier to breed from these colours, because if he
breeds a rabbit with grand markings, he will meet with
very little success in the show pen.

Next we come to greys, a colour I have taken great
interest in. Further, I have done not a little to bring
steel greys to their present pinnacle of fame. That they
are the most popular colour, and the best colour to wear,
there can be little doubt. The fact of their going a little
brown only intensifies their beauty. In this colour there
are two shades, steel grey and light grey, but the steel greys
are gradually and surely starving the light greys out of
existence. This no one will very much regret, but I shall
always contend that the light or brown greys bred with
distinct belly markings and stops should be put on the
same level as a steel grey if it is equal in markings, &c.
I shall not attempt here to advise how to produce steel greys,
because the colour has now become so fixed that it can be
transmitted to the progeny with great regularity, but I
should advise fanciers in starting this colour to get their
stock from those whom they know have bred their stock

from steel grey blood. In this colour the blacks must again be used, but you can often pair the steel greys together with admirable results. I have got as many as nine steel greys in one litter from this cross, but the blacks will have to be used sometimes to increase the density of grey. One thing I should like to draw special attention to in this colour is the bright steel ticking; this should be evenly distributed all over the head, ears, and body, making the grey one uniform shade. Many breeders have got the grey too dark, nearly black in places, especially on the back and cheeks. To my mind, this is a bad fault, and fanciers should ever bear in mind the advantage of having them with bright steel ticking. A cross with a blue will sometimes be found of great benefit, and, strange to say, " Eclipse " was bred from a steel grey doe by a blue buck, and his colour was really grand, although perhaps not so bright as some of the present day greys. The colour and ticking should always be maintained to its standard on the belly and hind feet, and any approach to light grey here is a defect, which shows the introduction of pale greys. Some very dark greys I have seen have had nearly white bellies and feet ; these are the wrong sort, because anyone's stock that has been carefully bred will not go so far astray as this. It is, no doubt, owing to pairing the steel and the light greys together—a cross I never recommend. In such a cross you introduce the very element you want to avoid.

The tortoise comes next, a colour over which there has been a good deal of contention. In my earlier days I

rather favoured as the standard of excellence, an approach
to the ideal, from which this colour derives its name,
tortoiseshell, and paid a lot of attention to breeding one to
my idea, but when I got the darker shades evenly distributed over the body, I must confess the result was
dismal and disappointing. The colours were not like those
of a Cavy, they were neither sharp nor clear enough, consequently they ran one into the other, and were not in any
way pleasing. I was, therefore, convinced that this
standard was neither desirable nor effective.

The other idea, and the one generally favoured, is
dark points round the edges of the cheek markings extending towards the eyes, the ears dark from the roots to the
points, also the haunches and hind feet. These densely
shaded blue-black points, with the other parts a nice sharp
deep yellow, is a blending both pleasing and effective, and,
after all, beauty is the idea that everyone should strive for,
although it seems strange that what is correct in a Cavy
or a Cat, is not the ideal for the same colour in a Rabbit.
This colour is best produced by crossing blacks with
them, and, except in the case of very dark parents, it is
not advisable to pair tortoiseshells together, they seem to
come soft in colour. Here, again, a blue can be paired to
a tortoise with advantage. It increases the density of the
shading very much, and often gets that desirable shade
which cannot be obtained without the adoption of the third
colour, because, after all, tortoise is a mixture of yellow,
black, and blue ; that is, of course, in reference to the
shading desirable on a Dutch Rabbit.

The other colour is yellow, but as the advantage of breeding such would, I feel sure, never repay the breeder, it is not necessary to enter into detail. Sufficient to say they must be entirely free from dark hairs round the smellers and haunches before they can be recognised as pure yellows ; otherwise, they are little better than bad tortoises. In fact, one can see that those shown of recent years have generally been produced more by accident from tortoises than from careful mating.

The blue fawns and blue greys are known as the off colours, and are not at all popular, consequently are seldom in the winning list against the other colours. I should, therefore, advise fanciers who intend breeding high-class Dutch, to avoid using these off colours in the breeding pen, as they are continually cropping up and spoiling the strain for breeding purposes.

If more attention was paid to colour in Dutch, I am sure we should get them much more beautiful than at present, which, when the markings were correct, would add greatly to their chances of success in the show pen. I know the first attempt may be disappointing, because, unless one knows how the parents have been bred, they cannot, with any degree of certainty, count on the success likely to attend their efforts. Perseverance will overcome all these little difficulties. Attention paid to breeding from good coloured specimens, and carefully mating them, wil amply repay the breeder.

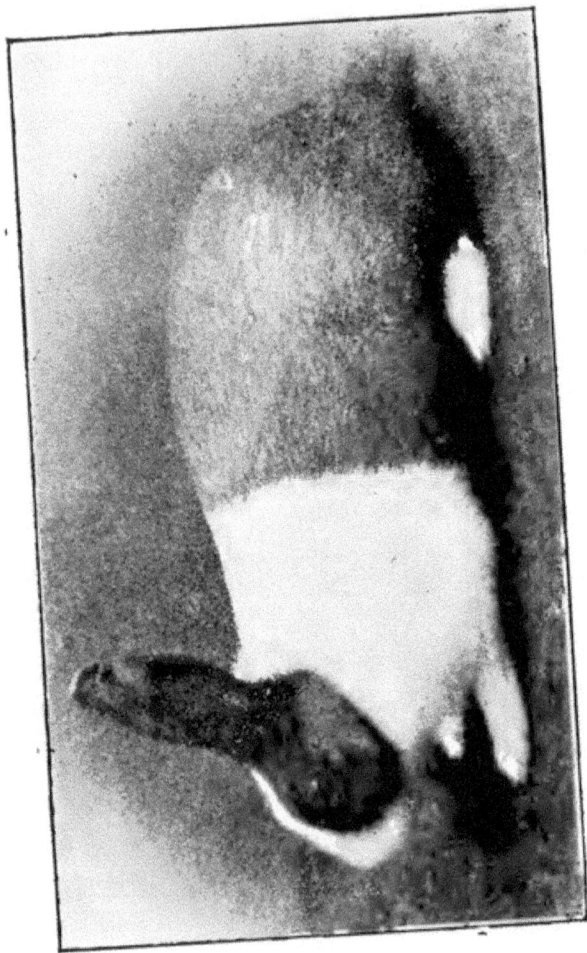

"Duchess," Tortoise Dutch Doe.

The property of Mr. R. J Jennings, Middlesbrough

Winner of 1sts and Specials Middlesbrough, 1895 and 1896, Newcastle, West Hartlepool, Haverton Hill, Perth, Cleveland, Haughton-le-Skerne, Crook, Wakefield, New Seaham, Ryhope, Blackhill, West Stanley, Arbroath.

CHAPTER IX.

Dutch, Past and Present.

In writing an appendix for this book, under the above heading, I should like to take this very favourable opportunity of acknowledging the great debt of gratitude that all fanciers of this most beautiful variety owe to Mr. Moss. No one, unless intimately associated with the working of specialist clubs, has any idea of the great amount of work that falls upon the shoulders of the secretaries, and to Mr. Moss must be attributed a large amount of credit to the present very flourishing condition of the Dutch Club, and also the variety that the club was promoted to foster.

My mission, however, in writing this appendix, is to recall memories of the past, and concentrate my readers' thoughts a little on the present day cracks. My knowledge of the past is, I know, not very extensive, as I cannot claim to be one of the old hands, but the results of research amongst the older records of the Dutch Fancy will, I hope, serve to make my contribution, at least, interesting reading.

In dealing with the past, I shall not attempt to inflict
upon my readers the tracing of the origin of the Dutch
Rabbit ; sufficient for my purpose to go back to the early
eighties, and review the worthies of those days.   The
illustration, representing the past, of a black and a tortoise, exhibited with very great success by Mr. Watmough, goes a
very long way to prove the great difference between the
winners of those days and the present day exhibition
specimens.   The marked improvement in shape is very
apparent from the picture.   The older representatives appear
very baggy and long in ears, the markings, too, exhibit a
striking example of the march of progress, as such markings as depicted here would, to-day, fail to get recognised
in a selling class.   This illustration forms a very pleasant
episode, linking, as it does, the old with the new, the past
with the present.

Fortunately, I am associated somewhat with experience
of the older Fancy by frequent pleasant chats I have had
with Messrs. Tottle, fellow-townsmen of mine at Bristol,
and the Dutch kings of days long since gone by ; men
who made Bristol famous in the days of yore with their
champions.   Those conversant with the Dutch Fancy
of those days will well remember the blacks, " La
Mode," " Marksman," " Lord Raglan," and " Black
Diamond " ;   the famous grey, " Grey Palmer," and
" Sunshine," the noted tortoise,   " Blue Skin," the
equally well-known Dutch, that derived its name from
its colour.

I have also listened with much chagrin and amuse-
ment of the lively doings of Dutch men in those days.
Trimming was, of course, a thing unknown, all were
penned as Nature formed them. No collusion with exhibitors and judges in those days of modesty and refinement.
Selling judges, their customers, agents, and such like only
existed in the imagination of some disappointed exhibitors.
All were interested in the best winning ; those who couldn't
trim didn't try, those who could didn't say so, but they
were done, nevertheless, and there were even recognised
mediums through which the process of preparation could
be done, and the matter was allowed to grow until it had
gained the upper hand ; but more anon on this—the vile
cancer of the Dutch Fancy.

Those days are days of old, gone never to return, only
in the minds of those who participated in the consequent
excitement and victory, and to bridge over the gulf existing
between the past and present, we must associate the names
of Messrs. Johnson, Enfield, Radford, Aconley, Outhwaite,
Gilpin, Potter, Gott, Brisley, Philps, Garlick, Ellis, Holroyd, Graham, and many others whose names do not
appeal to me at present. Some of these are like the
measles and bad weather, always with us, whilst others
crop up like the proverbial gooseberry, to demonstrate to
present day champions that the old hands have lost none
of their cunning.

One of the representatives of those days which did an
immense amount of winning was Outhwaite's " St. John,"

which won an enormous number of prizes, bringing us to
the period of those highly successful cracks, " Kingston
Gem " and " Kingston Princess." Those who remember
the black will always associate her name with lovely colour,
ears, and type, and really beautiful short coat.   This
exhibit, and the tortoise, generally accounted for first in
both classes, and the way which the genial Tommy
Holroyd always kept them in tip-top form, considering
how they were shown, speaks volumes for his knowledge
of the treatment of the sprightly little Dutchman.   Another
black of this period that caused a great sensation as a
youngster, was the one exhibited by that enthusiastic and
genial fancier, Mr. James Graham.   To know this fancier
is a pleasure, but to learn him is a most interesting pursuit.
I feel sure that what he doesn't know about a Dutch is not
worth learning.   This Rabbit was brought out towards the
end of 1890, and, after securing a large number of firsts,
was secured by Mr. Tottle for £12.   Its worst fault, to my
mind, was that its saddle was on the cross, but its shape,
colour, ears, and coat were everything to be desired.   Its
promising career was, however, cut short by its going
blind in one eye.

Then came the redoubtable tortoise, " Moonshine,"
which made the name of Sammy Pearson a household
word in the Dutch Fancy.   This Rabbit was, undoubtedly,
a grand all round exhibit, and probably the best tortoise
ever penned, his left cheek, full neck, and slight break on
top collar being his worst defects.   The one great feature

of this Rabbit, to my mind, was the really remarkable constitution he must have had, as I know of no Rabbit that did so much knocking about, and showed less signs of being over-shown than this famous tortoise, and up to the very last he always kept in really good coat. One thing, however, about this Rabbit that seemed most peculiar to me, considering what a great favourite he always was, was how very few specials he won for best Rabbit in the show. I well remember his being at Chesterfield, where there were four specials for best in show, and they were awarded as follows:—a Lop got special No. 1, a Belgian Hare No. 2, a Silver No. 3, and an Angora No. 4. However, all that has been avenged since, and Dutch have probably won more specials for best in show this last two or three years than any other variety. The same year we had the famous steel grey, " Eclipse," without a doubt the best grey penned up to that time, his colour was splendid, but he failed on one stop, was too wide at the bottom of the blaze, and too long in body to my liking. This Rabbit was bred by Mr. Johnson, of Kettering, and afterwards passed into my hands, and was shown by me with great success. I then sold him to Mr. Cooper at the then record price of fifteen pounds. He won a lot for this fancier, and at his death came into my possession again ; was then sold to Mr. Malley, for whom he won a great deal.

About the same time, I also bred and brought out the famous steel grey named " Grey Victor," without doubt the best Dutch for colour, ears, type, and sprightliness that

was ever penned, and probably the foundation of the
present-day steel greys. The success of this pair, was, no
doubt, the cause of so many fanciers getting the steel grey
fever, and about this time everybody went in for breeding
steel greys. Writing of " Grey Victor " reminds me of this
Rabbit's abominable temper. The notoriety which he
obtained for biting was equal to his success as a winner,
and the number of fanciers who bear testimony to his
industry with his teeth must be legion. Few exhibits had
a record superior to " Grey Victor,' and his activity was
truly phenomenal. I remember on one occasion sending
him to six different shows straight off the reel without
coming home, to see if tiring him out before coming home
would make him better tempered. His journeys from one
show to the other totalled over a thousand miles, but he
bit someone, so I afterwards learnt, at nearly every show.
The railway man who delivered him at the finish will always
have good cause to remember him as he bit the top of
his thumb off. In carrying the box, he put his thumb
through the ventilation hole, with the result that " Grey
Victor " bit the top clean off. This was the worst escapade
of this ever-memorable, yet pugnacious, Dutchman.

Leaving this period, and coming to 1893, brings us to
the sensational winner, " Magpie." That this exhibit had
a remarkable career, no one will deny. I always thought,
however, that she was a remarkably lucky Rabbit, and
although I may be accused of attempting to depreciate her
fame, it must be generally acknowledged that she had a

Mr. John Malley.

remarkable run of success, considering that she had so
many faults. About this time, the name of Mr. Malley
flashed across the annals of Dutch celebrities, and no
record of recent years would be complete without a word
of praise to this gentleman's unswerving fidelity to everything
best and purest in support of that breed which has made his
name a household word in the Rabbit Fancy. I remember
he had four very grand Dutch on the boards, " Climax,"
" Eclipse," " Pinate," and " Sunbeam "; " Climax " a
bonny tortoise, grand markings and type, but had to
contend against a speck on eye. " Eclipse " I have
already dealt with. " Pinate " was the black that
caused such a sensation by beating the unbeaten
" Magpie " at Grimsby, and caused such a spirited
discussion in *Fur and Feather*. I shall, however, always
consider " Pinate " the best black Dutch penned up
to this period ; her magnificent shape, ears, type, colour,
and almost perfect markings, with the most lovely short
coat of raven black hue I ever saw on a Dutch, constituted
to my mind the *beau ideal* of what a Dutch should be.
" Pinate " was bred by Mr. Ashby, of Northampton, was
claimed by me at Grimsby Show, and secured by
Mr. Malley, for whom she won about fifty first prizes.
" Sunbeam " was an excellent specimen of a steel
grey, had phenomenal success in the show pen, and
must have won nearly as many firsts as any Dutch
yet penned. Her worst faults were her stops and long
body. This doe was bred by Mr. Baxter, of Grimsby,
bought by me when a youngster, afterwards sold to

Mr. Malley, and was quite invincible for a long time in the Any Other Colour class. For some considerable time these rabbits won all before them, and the amount of winning they did grew almost monotonous.

The year 1895 brought that old and enthusiastic fancier Mr. James Graham to the front again, and the successes he achieved with the blacks. "Cleopatra" and "Yorkshire Lass" were both well merited and very popular ; they were grand in markings and colour, but both failed in shape. This, however, I fancy, was as much due to this popular fancier's liberal diet as anything else. Another black that he did well with, and which was bred by a very deservedly respected fancier, Mr. Pollard, of Bath, was "Lord Nelson," the black which won the Sheffield Fanciers' Young Cup in 1894, and was bought after spirited competition at the auction by Mr. Aconley, afterwards passed into the hands of Mr. Stead, who was very successful with him, thence into the hands of Mr. Graham. This was a really good Dutch, but he got coarse, and his colour did not last. Another, with which Mr. Graham did a great deal of winning, was the tortoise buck. This rabbit's odd face, a fault so apparent, told greatly against his general character ; still his other grand markings and colour helped him to win a large number of firsts.

Mr. Moss, too, this last two years, has been showing some good blacks, his cup winner at Lincoln in 1895 being a bonny exhibit, her worst fault was her short

stops, her success after this being fairly well maintained.
Then in 1896 at Leamington, he again won the cup with
a recent purchase, Mr. Graham's " Yorkshire Lass,"
the doe's lovely condition on this occasion helping her
immensely.

Another name, the owners of which have won a large
number of prizes in Dutch during the last three or four
years, is Wallis—the Messrs. Wallis and Son, of
Cambridge. One very successful rabbit was the grey
disqualified at Lincoln in 1896, and which the Investigation
Committee of the Dutch Club exonerated. This rabbit
afterwards passed into the hands of Mr. Minkley, whose
name will always be kindly thought of by Dutch fanciers
as the pioneer of the Sheffield Dutch Show. With this
gentleman he did well. The rabbit was undoubtedly a
good one, but like so many other good marked ones, he
was too large. Another very successful Dutch of Messrs.
Wallis' was the blue that won the Dutch Club Cup
at Leamington in 1896. This rabbit was, no doubt, one
of the best of its colour ever penned, grandly marked
all round, and sound in colour, with exceptionally nice
ears. This firm also had a black out some two or more
years ago that was of wonderful type and markings, but
very brown in colour, otherwise I think it would have
made itself very famous.

This brings us to 1896—a year of great success
for my favourite colour, steel greys. The success of
Mr. Malley's pair " Hoghton Grey Laddie " and " Hoghton

Grey Lassie" was indeed very remarkable. The former was, to my mind, a really grand exhibit but its small cheek markings must have told against it; still, in equal condition, I thought it superior to any Dutch of the year. Its ears, type, colour, neck, collar, cut, and stops being about perfect. "Grey Lassie" was not so good in shape or markings, and was not ticked even enough with the bright steel ticking. The champion specials for best in show that these two accounted for during the year was, I think, the best up to date. The end of the year brought us that grand steel grey of Mr. Adcock's, claimed by Mr. Graham at Rochester, and which turned the tables on "Hoghton Grey Laddie" at Stratford-on-Avon the week after, also securing the special for best in show—a feat he has done so many times since. This rabbit is no doubt, of wonderful shape, has good colour, ears, eyes, saddle, cut, and stops, but his face is, to my mind, a very long way from being right, and his neck is very full. He, no doubt, wants a lot of handling to be appeciated, but his type, colour, and style is of the highest order.

Another rabbit for which I predict a very successful career is a young black penned this year by Mr. Malley, and which got second in a very large class at Northampton. At this show it was getting into full coat, and I think when fully made up, it will take all the best to stop it. It has grand face, neck, collar, and stops, and the best type and colour I have seen for a long time. At

Northampton it was wavy on collar, the new coat not having grown sufficient to show its true quality. This, I think, concludes a review of most of the leading Dutch of the present, and if I have grown tedious, I must apologise to my readers.

CHAPTER X.

Type and Trimming.

There are one or two other features relating to this comparison of the present with the past that I should like to allude to, and that is the marked tendency among our leading judges to improve the type of our winning Dutch. Many may think that judges are not the ones from whom we must expect improvement, but like everything else, the demand creates the supply, and those who know anything about exhibition life, know well that the great secret of success is " to tickle the judge's fancy." This may be considered a very vulgar phrase, but everyone knows that if judges are demanding, by their awards, improvement in any particular direction, that quality will certainly be forthcoming, and those who know that the large coarse Dutch are being dropped because of their bad shape, at once set about putting their breeding arrangements in order, so that they may correct the bad points which judges are setting their faces against. That Dutch have improved in shape no one will deny, but I am hoping that we shall get them a lot shorter in the back and couplings, short limbs of finer bone, and smaller heads with thin and short ears.

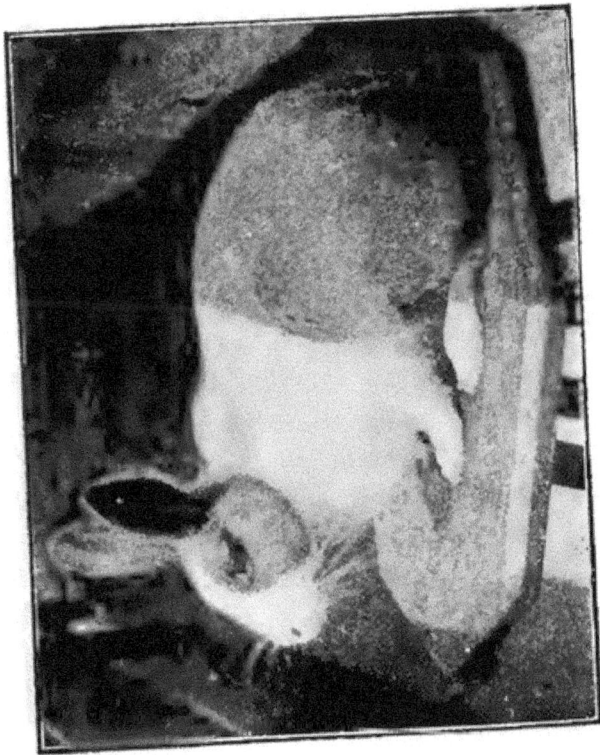

"Flying Dutchman," Blue Dutch Buck.

The property of Mr. H. Dowson, Eagley, Bolton.

Winner of 1st and Medal Stockport, 1st Eagley, and many other prizes.

I may say that it is a great fallacy on the part of some to think that size in Dutch is governed by feeding; improvement must come by choice of parents in the direction indicated above ; get them with these points, and, carefully mated and judiciously fed, and no fear need be felt of their getting too large. My experience of Dutch is that they must be shown in nice condition as regards flesh to show off their markings to advantage, because if they lack flesh their markings are always more or less wavy; this particularly applies to the collar.

I may add that one cannot decide the type of Dutch by the application of the weight principle. A Dutch under five pounds is not of necessity good type, nor is one over five pounds necessarily bad type. Still, I like them of a size and shape that would, if they answered my idea, never exceed this limit. The great feature, however, in a Dutch will always be its markings, and whilst great attention has been paid to the other points, marking is still the fascinating feature, and the reason of their popularity. On this point I should like to make a few references as to Dutch being penned in a perfectly natural state. I know there are some who think it an impossibility to win successfully without trimming. This is altogether misleading as I am positive that several of our most successful Dutch of recent years have never been touched, and if it were not that I might be thought partial, I could name those who pen their stock in a perfectly natural state.

In respect to this question of trimming, I claim to be one of the leaders of the crusade against trimming, and I may say that since such was started, the Dutch Club has been most successful. Dutch have been shown far more honestly than hitherto, and they have realised far higher prices, a test which proves that fanciers are prepared to pay large amounts, if they are certain they are buying an honest specimen.

To anyone who has had any experience with a question of this kind, it will be a natural sequence. It involved a very large amount of labour to cripple this vile tumour, which had grown to such an extent that faking a few years back had got the upper hand, and it was very difficult to suggest an effectual remedy. The Investigation Committee has, generally speaking, done its work well, and if our judges only act fearlessly, I am sure that faking will never grow to the extent it attained hitherto. Fashion rules most things, and strange to say, fashion had deeply rooted an impression in the minds of many that Dutch were trimmed, that to win it was necessary to trim, and judges having let trimming get the upper hand, were scarcely able to make up their minds how and where to suppress it. To blame the judges was shifting the responsibility on to the shoulders of those who were not the offenders, and they did not care to incur a life-long displeasure, because by disqualifying an exhibit, they branded its owner as being guilty of dis- honest practices.

I am pleased to say that all this has been changed, the judges, or a majority of them, disqualifying all those exhibits not shown naturally, whilst the owners have the right to appeal against the decisions, and also of giving an explanation to the Dutch Club Committee.

However, of trimming, I may say, that the tumour has been cut out roots and all, and I feel sure that present day fanciers will never allow it to grow again. I would urge all to nip it in the bud by assisting those who are doing their best to rid the Fancy of this unwholesome pest. If fanciers will only buy honest exhibits, and set their faces against prepared and worthless specimens, the faker will die a natural death. There is no honour, surely, in a prize won with a specimen that has been made to exhibit points of excellence it never naturally possessed. The position is a debasing lie, and let us hope, for the the sake of one of the prettiest exhibition rabbits, that it will continue to be shown honestly and fairly. Don't blame the judges. Their task is a very unthankful one, and I know that I have made innumerable enemies over disqualification. My reply has always been that the enemies I had made, and so-called friends I had lost, I could do very well without. I have no sympathy with those who countenance dishonest practices because such are fashionable, and I have a perfect hatred of those, who, having won prizes with worthless specimens, turn and abuse judges with that scurrility that is only equalled by their love of ill-gotten gain. I remember writing the above sentence in 1893, and now nearly four years after, the trimming brigade has been crippled, and what do we find ? Why, Dutch are winning specials for best in show oftener than any other variety. This proves that there is not the slightest necessity to trim them to secure recognition at the hands of our judges. I always claim that any man who can breed live stock where markings are the chief characteristics, to a near approach to perfection, and maintain the other good points such as size, shape, colour, carriage, &c., deserves all the encouragement that can possibly be given him, especially when the exhibits are penned honestly.

I must ask my readers' indulgence in extending this part of my treatise so long, but so much depends upon this question of trimming, and its wretched consequences if allowed to grow is my only excuse for so doing.

One other point that I should like to refer to is faulty eyes. This question is continually cropping up, and the most frequent is specks. Now, to my mind, the eyes should be perfectly free from any discolouration whatever, and in all cases take the exact colour of its coat. I have always held the opinion that the trouble arises from crossing the various colours, and at times using wall-eyed Dutch in the breeding pen. I should advise fanciers to rigorously avoid using rabbits in the mating pens that have this defect, as no fault is so faithfully transmitted to the progeny as unsound eyes, and once it gets into a stock, it is continually cropping up, and generally in the best marked ones. Another defect that looks like causing considerable trouble is wrong coloured eyes, and generally arises in blacks having eyes that are properly coloured for a rabbit of a tortoise colour. This is not easily noticeable, but at first it looks unnatural, and on close examination, of course, very much so, and is, to my mind, a great defect. One or two noted Dutch occur to my mind that had this serious defect. One was a black exhibited by Mr. A. Moore, for which report has it £18 was paid ; be this as it may, it no doubt prevented this doe leading as she would have done. Another still more recent occurence was a black exhibited by Messrs. Thompson and Harland.

With this review of past and present I must close this, I fear, not very interesting chapter, and I hope the few remarks may prove encouraging to those who are helping by their endeavours to foster the advancement of the Dutch Fancy.

www.ingramcontent.com/pod-product-compliance
Lightning Source LLC
Chambersburg PA
CBHW020327090426
42735CB00009B/1429